FROM A PEBBLE
TO A ROCK

*Life stories from the home front
to encourage the hearts of every woman*

Patti A. Correa

xulon
PRESS

Contents

Acknowledgments

My Lord and Savior Jesus Christ for his blessings on this journey.

My husband, Ed and son, Kyle, I love you.

My mother, thank you for all those special mother/daughter talks.

Francis Warner for the beautiful illustration dedicated to moms and wives of those who have served or currently serving our country. (www.franart.com)

Pastor Tommy, for your encouragement and wisdom.

Lyna, my editor and friend, without whom this book would not be completed.

Melanie, thanks for helping me meet the deadlines.

Special thanks and blessing to those who have served or are serving our country. May God keep you safe and bless you.

To all those who have had any part in helping me on this journey. Thank you.

Foreword

Get set for some interesting reading as you pursue these heart-warming stories Patti Correa has put together of the wives and mothers of some of our military men.

If we're not careful we tend to overlook or even forget those women who stay behind while their spouses and sons go far away to other places for assignments or perhaps action. Day by day these ladies face the pain of loneliness, their own heavier responsibilities, and the anxious uncertainty that accompanies this particular kind of separation.

Patti keeps us from not seeing them! She brings into sharp focus the trials as well as the joys of these loved ones of our troops who are left to wait patiently while their men serve our country, often in far-removed locations.

It's been my privilege to be Patti's pastor for several years. I knew she had a kinship with military families because of her experiences with a dad and a husband, but the tender, compassionate way she digs out these narratives confirms my beliefs that she has a sensitive, gracious heart for these women and wants to be a blessing to them. You'll enjoy, and be refreshed by this book.

Two scripture verses come to mind. In Romans 12:15 Paul directs us to "rejoice with those who rejoice and weep with those who are weak." The ladies in these vignettes have their share of both of those emotions and it's our great opportunity to pray for them and reach out to them in helpful assistance.

Then, in Psalm 30:5 the ancient writer reminds us that "weeping may endure for a night, but joy comes in the morning." We are so greatful that most of our guys get to return home to their families. Our hearts ache for those homes where, because of death, there will be a permanent absence. But in any case, because of God's providence, we know a day is coming when there will be no more war and thus no real need for soldiers to journey far away. Praise the Lord!

Thanks, Patti, for alerting us to the fact that, in the meantime, we should make an extra effort to get to know and share our concern for these ladies who wait hopefully.

Pastor Tommy Davidson
Newport News, VA

Dedicated to all the women whose Sailors, Soldiers, Airmen and Marines have served or are serving our country in the United States Armed Forces.

Proverbs 31:25-27
She is clothed with strength and dignity, and can laugh at the days
to come. She speaks with wisdom, and faithful instruction is on her
tongue. She watches over the affairs of her household and does not
eat the bread of idleness. Her children arise and call her blessed;
her husband also, and he praises her; "Many women do noble
things but you surpass them all."

NIV

Introduction

My dad left approximately two weeks before I was born for an 8-month assignment in Italy with the U.S. Navy. After my dad found out he was leaving he began taking my mom for car rides over hills and bumps, in an attempt to coerce my early arrival into the world. Unfortunately for him I was already sampling the waters of disobedience and refused to comply for another two weeks. I was 8 months old before my dad first laid eyes on me. He was in the Navy and serving our country in 1962 during the Cuban Crisis on the USS Beale. The first time he saw me we had gone to meet his ship as it came in to Norfolk, Virginia. Mom carried me in her arms to meet my dad. There were so many sailors my mom could not find my dad. But he saw us. He took me in his arms and welcomed me. In 1963, my brother was born and he was three days old when my dad saw him. Back in the day when hitchhiking was safe my dad hitchhiked from Norfolk, Virginia to Minneapolis, Minnesota to see his son and family. My mom tells me stories of hardship and sacrifices that were made while my dad was in the Navy. Unfortunately the separation time was too great for my parent's marriage to survive. There were no support groups like there are today. My dad has said that when he came home it was like coming home to a stranger. So at the age of nine, my parents were divorced. I renewed my relationship with my father 22 years later. Since then I have learned so much about what he did in the military and have grown

so very proud of him. Dad has told me there were times when he did not know if he would ever see me again. He could not call home because he was on a ship out at sea. He said mail would come by helicopter and bags filled with mail would be lowered to the deck along with an empty one attached and sent back up to the helicopter. The helicopter would then fly away to the states with letters of love. My mom would send him pictures of me as a baby. If I had not renewed my relationship with my dad I would not have learned how he served our country and how much he loves me. Since then I have learned so much about- this man- my Dad- and also his service to our country. Just recently we laughed and shared memories that I never knew happened.

One of the greatest hardships my mom faced during his tours at sea was when the military pay checks were delivered by mail and would often get delayed or sometimes even lost. We needed food in the house. My mom told me of a time when she went to a small local store in our neighborhood that a little Jewish storekeeper owned and asked him if she could charge a few little things. He told her to go ahead and get a few things. As she went to the counter he told her to go ahead that there would be no charge. After all those years my mom still remembers that little Jewish man who helped our family.

Over the past 60 years there is one thing that has remained constant - the roller coaster of emotions often times felt by women whose soldiers have been deployed overseas or away at war. For these women the road is never smooth thrust into the role of a single parent while their soldier is away defending our country. But then, we are to be reminded that our soldiers are sacrificing their lives for our freedom and our country's freedom. The role of women on the homefront has not changed except that life is much busier now. The load that is carried is just as difficult now as it was then. The home must go on, the bills must be paid, and the children must be cared for. During WWII the only means of communication with their soldiers were by letters. Women would listen to the radio and only hear a portion of what was going on. The only real way they would know what was going on was by letters from their soldiers. Today we have email, cell phones and the mail is actually a little faster.

With today's technology and news media we often know what is going on before our soldiers do. I truly admire the strength of women on the homefront. Women who over the years have made many sacrifices. Women who keep the homefront going all the while not knowing whether their soldier is coming home. I often imagine a woman holding a letter from her soldier close to her heart and would read it whenever she was lonely.

During WWII V-mail became a very popular tool to correspond with a soldier serving overseas. V-mail became even more popular between 1942 and 1944. V-mail consisted of miniature messages reproduced by microphotography from 16mm film. The system was designed to use a special V-mail letter sheet, which was combined with the envelope. The user would write a short message in the limited space provided, adding the name and address of the person receiving the message. The letter was then put into the specially marked envelope and mailed. The V-mail was then reduced to thumbnail size on microfilm. One roll of film weighing about 7 ounces could hold over 1,500 letters. The rolls of film were then flown across the world and developed at a destination closest to the person receiving the mail. Finally, individual facsimiles of the V-mail letter were mailed and delivered. The V-mail system reduced the amount of time a soldier waited to receive mail and made it possible to receive news from their loved ones and soldiers in less than a month. V-mail was very compact. You could think of this as the early beginnings of e-mail. (**www.merkki.com/dson5.htm**). Today's technology allows us to communicate with our soldier in many ways. We have email, more frequent phone calls and video cameras. The soldiers can now purchase and use cell phones while serving across the world.

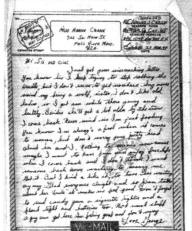
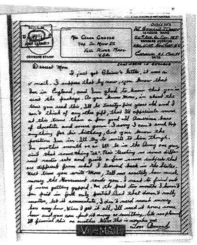

Stories

As the military spouse or mom of a soldier, the road often begins with uncertainty, fear and sometimes loss. As we grow through the years our lives become more grounded, a refuge for support, and an encouragement to others. Join me in a journey as women tell their stories of hope and strength through times of war and separation and how they grew from a pebble to a rock. May these stories encourage your hearts and make times of separation a little easier.

Amanda

As I spoke with Amanda on the phone I could hear in her voice the pride she has for her husband. Amanda is a new military wife and stationed with her husband, Nathan, at Fort Benning, GA. He has been in the Army for two years. One week after they were married Nathan went off to boot camp. He missed the birth of his son, Gavin, but saw him two weeks later.

Nathan recently served in Iraq as a tank mechanic with the 3rd Infantry Division (3rd ID). Nathan left in January of 2003 and returned home in June 2003. Nathan communicated by phone to his wife while in Kuwait. He was there for about 30 days before heading into Iraq. Once in Iraq there was no communication except by letter which could take up to 30 days to arrive. Some of her letters he never received. Both were frustrated with not being able to communicate as much. Being a new mother and military wife Amanda went to Virginia to be with her family and receive support from loved ones. Even though she was away from Georgia she still watched the news wondering about her husband. Some nights she would stay up all night and watch the news. Finally, she had to turn it off because of the stress and worry for her soldier.

Amanda dealt with the separation by videotaping her son and taking pictures. She visited with Nathan's family, which made her feel closer to her soldier. Once a week she would send a care package to him filled with cigarettes, letters, snacks and pictures. Nathan took many pictures but could not get them developed until he came home. While her soldier was away she moved into a new house and had to move all their things from storage to their new house. She did have the help of three of her girlfriends.

The reality of war really set in for Amanda when Nathan called from Kuwait and said they were moving into Baghdad and he would not be able to call her for awhile. She then realized how real war is. Amanda is experiencing the newness of being a military wife, realizing all too well that her soldier is gone quite a bit whether it be a deployment or war. As for Gavin, he was too young to experience the emotion of a child missing his daddy. But when he saw his daddy, he smiled.

Brenda

Sitting across from Brenda in the den of her home I saw the strength of a woman filled with such love and respect for her soldier, even after 35 years of marriage. Brenda was barely 20 when she married Cary. Her family did not want her to get married too soon out of fear that if something should happen to her soldier. So they waited. So miserable and desperately wanting to be together she got married three weeks before her soldier left for Vietnam in April of 1969. Both families were very supportive and knew they had made the right decision. Brenda just knew she had to be her soldier's wife before he went to war.

As newlyweds it was hard to separate. Being separated during awful circumstances was hard. Not having the chance to live together and get to know each other that first year was tough. Phone calls were difficult at times. Short wave HAM radios were used. Talking and listening were two separate functions that could not be done at the same time. When they spoke to each other one must listen and must have their radio in listen mode and when one person finished he must say "over" for the other person to know to change the handset to talk. Her soldier would have to sign up to use the radio. Brenda says it was very expensive but so good to hear his voice on the other end.

The most difficult time was when Cary was sent to the field one week out of each month. She had no idea where he was going. There was no communication at all. She was always apprehensive that one week out of each month when he would go out amongst the enemy.

Brenda was happy when the American Red Cross would let her and the family come to record a message to him. His mother and father would record a message and then would leave the room and Brenda would record her personal message to her soldier. She would update him on all the happenings at home. Red Cross would then send it to get to the soldier. Letters were the only real form of communication. She wrote letters daily. While he was in Vietnam she would go to her room and play record albums of love songs. He wrote when he could and Brenda would often get a group of letters at a time. As she received the letters she would put them in date order so she could read them over and over. Brenda stayed involved with friends and family while her soldier was gone. She wrote a lot of poems to him which she still has today along with every letter he ever wrote her.

One of her most memorable times was when she turned 21. For her birthday her husband made arrangements with his mother to buy her a piece of luggage so she could use it when she met her soldier for some Rest and Relaxation (R and R). "He went through a lot of trouble to make sure I had that," Brenda said. "He wrote a nice card saying how turning 21 was so special and how he was sad he could not be there." The first care packages Brenda sent Cary took three months to get to him. She sent the basics: candy, home-made cookies, peanuts, socks, deodorant, licorice and Kool-Aid to mask the bad taste of the water.

Brenda said she was too young and did not realize what could happen on a day-to-day basis. But she is a very optimistic person. She was working while Cary was in Vietnam and when she drove to work every morning she would look at the sun rising, thinking, "This is a very beautiful day and my husband is looking at it from a totally different perspective." Brenda would often play music and cope that way. She had family to help support her. While her husband was serving in Vietnam Brenda was dealing with her dad and his health. He had lung cancer. Brenda truly believes he was waiting to die to make sure she was going to be okay. He died three weeks after her husband returned from Vietnam.

Brenda showed me the picture that her husband still carries in his wallet. It is his favorite picture of her. It is a picture of them on their wedding day. He is in his uniform and she is as beautiful as every bride is. The picture is faded, wrinkled and weathered after being in his wallet for so many years. He loved the picture so much he hired a Korean to paint a portrait of it and paid ten dollars to have it done. Today, that portrait hangs on the wall of their living room. Brenda has kept all his uniforms, awards and medals.

Brenda has never regretted the decision to marry because she knew in her heart it was right for them. The hardships they lived through that first year were worth it. Brenda offers these encouraging words to other spouses, "If you have made a commitment to your soldier, go with your heart and take each day as it comes, find something positive in each day. Learn and grow while your loved one is away so when he comes back you will have more to love and grow together. Know your heart and go for it! don't let things sway you. Be true to each other." Brenda says that spouses, who depend on their husband for everything, make it harder on themselves to put one foot in front of the other as an individual.

As with any military spouse, the hardest part is to see your soldier go back to the war zone after some R&R. She told me that when she went to the airport, on one side would be a line of women waiting for their spouses to return for good and on the other side were those saying goodbye. She will never forget when it was her turn to be on the other side, welcoming her soldier home. She wore a vivid pink dress and says when he saw her he scooped her up in his arms and they headed home.

Sylvia

Speaking with Sylvia just made my heart leap. To hear the pride and patriotism in her voice was wonderful. Her soldier, Bill served for 23 years. Sylvia recalls moving many times during his time of service. Bill was in the Army and served in both the Korean War and Vietnam War. "I sent him two letters every day. One letter was to catch him up on everything going on around the house. The second one was to tell him all about our two year-old-son" Sylvia said. Bill served in Vietnam in 1965 with the 11th Air Assault as a helicopter pilot and was in the air flying all the time. Sylvia said that her soldier never talked much about the war but she does remember him saying that, "He flew anything from cows to people."

During Bill's first tour in Vietnam she would send letters. She rarely got to speak to him on the phone. When he came home after one year she didn't recognize his voice. "It was such a shock not recognizing my husband's voice." As I heard this I could not believe it. We are so fortunate with today's technology. Our soldiers now have cell phones in the field. Determined not to forget his voice again, on his second tour she sent him audio tapes of all the sounds of home – car horns, kids, running water, and the ticking of a clock. He would also send audio tapes. She was always so excited to hear his voice. Sylvia still has those tapes today. They are marked for her children to listen to, especially for her grandson to listen to his Grandfather while he fought for his country.

Bill's second tour in Vietnam came just 18 months later. Six months after beginning his second tour in Vietnam he was able to have some rest and relaxation in Hawaii. Sylvia met him there. Sending him back was the most difficult part. As they parted, she wondered if she would see him again.

He didn't talk much about his tours. One story she remember him telling her was one of her favorites. He told her while they were landing a helicopter in Vietnam they heard guns shooting all over.

He thought "this is it, I'm going down." Once it quieted down it turned out to be a soldier shooting at a big snake. That was one of her favorite memories.

One of the biggest things Sylvia feels Bill missed out on was the children growing up. When he returned home Sylvia was blessed to see that there were no real changes in Bill. She recalls one time they were getting in the car to go somewhere and she went to the driver's side without any hesitation. Her husband asked "What are you doing?" She remembers laughing and realized that you get into habits and forget and have to readjust all over again.

Sylvia would always work in the yard. There were times when she would see an Air Force car go past and under her breath would pray, "please, don't stop here." She still remembers all those emotions and gets teary eyed when they come back. Being both parents was challenging. If something went wrong on the homefront it could take three weeks to a month to get a response from her soldier. So she often made the decisions on her own.

I asked Sylvia what got her through that time of war. "I had a good married life, peace in my heart, and I thank God I had Bill for 29 years." The number one thing that got her through was prayer. She became a stronger person and appreciated her husband so much more. I asked Sylvia what words of encouragement she would pass on to another spouse. "Keep a stiff upper lip. Be strong for the family and not for yourself. Put self aside and be strong."

Mildred

Mildred remembers WWII. Her husband served three years in WWII. She remembers letters by mail which could take up to a month. She would receive letters by V-Mail. She checked mail each day looking for a letter from her soldier. News of the war would be heard on radio. She said "you wouldn't hear too much. Especially like you hear it today."

The birth of their first child was in 1943. He received the message of his first born by an American Red Cross message. He saw his first child for 5 days in 1944 and then for 5 days in 1945.

January, 1946 her soldier came home. Mildred says her husband wasn't the same man when he came home. But they survived it all. Her husband has been dead for 18 years.

Mildred was around family during the time her husband was away. So the support of the family helped alot. Then the Vietnam War. Her two sons and son-in-law served in Vietnam. Her sons served two years. She was concerned about her sons every day. They made it home safely.

I asked Mildred what words of encouragement she could offer another military spouse. "Take one day at a time and send packages to your soldier."

Irene

This life story comes from a daughter's eyes. A daughter who cries at the sound of a patriotic song, a daughter who saw her mom as a rock in their family. This is the story of a family that experienced a tragic loss, gained tremendous strength and family bonding. I sat with Irene and was so impressed with the love and respect she has for her mom. Irene has her own family now with a husband and three boys. She speaks of her mom with great pride. While her dad was away serving our country she remembers her mom making sure the kids had food, clothing, shoes. Irene says, "Oftentimes it may not have been the food or things we wanted, but we survived, she took care of us". She showed me pictures of her family.

Her dad, Fernando, is a Black Hawk helicopter pilot with the U.S. Army and has been in the military for 37 years. He left in February 2003 to serve in Iraq. Irene's sister is also in Iraq. She is in the U.S. Air Force and left for Iraq in March 2004. When Fernando knew his daughter had arrived he went to see her but she was not at her tent. He left her a note. He returned the next day and saw his daughter. She was so overwhelmed to see him she did not want to let him go.

Irene remembers her mother doing everything while her dad was away during times of war or deployment. Her mother mowed the lawn, cooked. She did everything. Irene remembers when she was young listening to her mother cry at night. "She never thought we could hear her", Irene said. "She was concerned for her soldier and raising her children".

Irene spoke of the military life, saying, "We are special and no matter what we are always connected to military life." She says she remembers her mother worrying a lot. She would watch the news all the time and when a helicopter went down she was scared to death. One thing that stood out the most while talking with Irene was the death of her brother, Fernando, Jr. He was 32 years old when he died in June of 2003. His dad was away serving when Fernando got sick. Her mother took care of her son all by herself while her husband was away. The sacrifices that were made were endless. While he was sick his dad went to Iraq. As he left for Iraq he asked his son if he was going to be his scout and Fernando said, "No, not this time, Dad." But before he died Fernando told his mom to tell his dad that he was coming to be his scout. Her brother served in the Navy for four years on the U.S.S. Saratoga in Florida.

Irene shared with me a letter that her dad wrote to his children from Iraq at Christmas 2003. As I read the letter, tears swelled up in my eyes. I could see the love expressed from a father to his children telling them that he loves them with all his heart and soul, wrote of himself as a part of the script that gave them life, but that his part in their creation was not as strong as their mother's. From the moment they were conceived in their mother's womb, part of him and her gave them life. Their mother's flesh and blood cradled and nourished them until the moment of their birth. His duty to his family was to love and take care of them.

The memory of Fernando Jr. will live on. He taught his family how valuable and fragile life is. Never take life for granted. During the last year of his life, he was blind. Speaking of his son he wrote, "Despite his blindness and the dark world he was living in, the many tears that filled his eyes and sadness that spilled from his heart, he was not convinced of his terminal illness. His will to live and someday return to normal was so strong that he would not give up and accept his fate. To see him like that only broke his mom's heart and saddened her soul. We all could see his pain and suffering. Mom saw it, felt and lived it. She helplessly comforted and nursed him every second of his life."

Irene's dad spoke of his family and how they are to always be there for each other. He referred to Christmas 2003 as a new beginning for all. He told his family that they are fortunate to have their other brother and sister next to them. He tells them to hug each other often and tell them that you love them. Fernando Jr was a D.J. and his father says that he is smiling and broadcasting Heaven's radio station. He closes his letter with tears of joy and praying it touches their hearts. "For it is from my heart to yours", he says. In closing he wishes his family a very Merry Christmas and Happy New Year. While in Iraq, Irene's mom sent a photo album of Fernando Jr., from birth until his last days. He says he is at peace when he looks at the album. One of the last things Irene said to me was that if she could go back in time, she would tell her family she loves them more and appreciates them. I asked Irene even after experiencing all the good and bad times of military life, what words would she offer another spouse.

"It is going to seem like it's going to rain alot but there will be sunny days ahead."

Linda

Sitting among memories dating back to 1942, Linda tells me the story of her father and his time serving our country. He loved helicopters more than anything in the world. He served in U.S. Army Air Corp and then went into the U.S. Air Force. Among the items Linda has kept was a card with his serial number that was used during his service time. To date, her father still remembers his number. Many pictures, awards, commendations, newspaper articles. Air Force 17 Feb 1943. 201 files which contained all his personal and career information on it and carried with him to every duty station, training, medals, army commendation medals (ARCOMs). Linda remembers moving about every 2 years. Her father never got rid of anything. Linda grew up in the military life with her siblings born all across the world. Linda then married into the military life.

Linda's father met her mother in Newfoundland. Linda was the first child born in the United States. Her mother was always involved in things. Linda rings true the old saying, "If the Army wanted you to have a wife, they would have issued you one." When she was growing up she says it was literal. Her mom never learned to drive. Other military wives would help out and had their own system of helping each other. All her brothers and sisters were involved in sports.

Linda says she always knew when her dad deployed they never knew his exact location, he was "just out." Many times this would present a problem. In those days he would not get paid like the soldiers do today. He was paid in cash. He would travel with his 201 file and his pay record just like it was a report card. She remembers living in Maine and coming home from school one day and her dad told her to go back to school and tell them she would be leaving tomorrow, they were getting packed for a move the next day.

She remembers her mom traveling with her brother because he was sick with asthma and her mom would get on a plane to Germany. She would be with friends or her sister would watch them. Mom could be at the hospital for weeks until her brother was well enough to come home.

Her dad served 28 years in the military. After 28 years he stood the risk of going to Vietnam. So her mom said, "Nope, that is enough." So he retired to North Carolina.

Linda met her husband at Fort Bragg and continued the military way of life. Linda married her husband and her husband joined the Army in Jan 1970 and retired in Jan. 2000. He served as an Intel in Infantry operations and then later changed to a Chaplain Assistant.

He experienced Desert SHIELD/STORM with the 18th Airborne Corp in December. While there he received a battlefield promotion. His promotion was videotaped so his wife could see it since she was not able to be there.

One of her most memorable memories of her father was when her mother use to always tell her that she would cry, cry, and cry when her dad was gone. Her mom would spank her and then Linda would tell her mom, "I'm going to tell my daddy." Everyone around them lived the same way and it was normal for them. They knew no other way of life. Wives and children would get together and everyone would bring something and have big meals and do things.

She remembers when they were living in Spain and her dad got to come home for two days. She remembers him walking in and saying, "Dad's home." "Daddy, daddy, daddy" she would yell.

Her sisters tell her she is more like him and was always playing with his tools. She remembers being on the flight line with him in Illinois when he was converting helicopters for civilian use. Watching him when they had a plane come down and had to put out the foam for the plane to land. She never considered the military life different. It was all she knew. She remembers very few times that her dad would call growing up. If there was an emergency another family that had a phone would come and get them. She remembers when her grandfather died and the Military Police delivered a telegram to her house.

Linda relates another childhood story from when her family was living in Spain. Her dad would put shortening on their feet and lift them up under the arms and place them on a paper bag to determine the size of their feet to order new shoes from the Sears catalog. They did not go to a Post Exchange store like we have today; there was a very small store and she remembers a tractor trailer going around the housing area. She remembers when she was eleven or twelve years-old and was so excited about getting a pair of shoes she wanted so badly with a heel. When she got them they were too small and she had to give them to her sister. She really wanted those shoes.

Linda has learned from her experiences as a child and a military spouse to stockpile. You always buy extra. If you know Christmas is coming you buy sugar, if you need chocolate chips you buy them. She remembers her mom doing all that when she was a child and has continued the tradition.

Linda finds herself moving things around frequently and feels antsy at times, feeling like she has to move. As a military spouse Linda had a tough time understanding why other women were crying all the time. She thinks growing up in a military environment has helped her to cope with separations. The military life has shaped her by making her very adaptable. It has exposed her to the world. She has traveled all her life and is thankful for the opportunity. She is able to pick up languages and culture very well. It has been a blessing to help others new to the United States and help them to overcome language barriers. It takes unique people to do it. You don't go into it saying, "I am going to do it for a little while" she says. "Be adaptable. You can have a great time. There is a whole world out there."

She knew women who would cry and stay in their apartments all day. It was hard on them and their husbands. "When you marry a soldier you have to understand. deployments are hard. You do what you gotta do and take it day by day and minute by minute." Linda's middle name is Ruth and like the Biblical heroine, believes you leave your father and mother when you marry. "When you marry somebody..."where thou goest I will go."

She encourages others to get out and get involved with support groups, community. Do what you can do where you are at. Help each other. Linda was active in speaking to Congress on behalf of saving the commissaries.

Linda and her husband reach out to those in need. Along the way, they have helped other military families. Linda was an American Red Cross volunteer and one time met a woman and a child. The child was in a full cast from the waist down. Linda felt she had to be there for this mother and child. The mother and child had nowhere to stay but the hospital and needed other things. Linda and her husband welcomed her to stay with them for a few days.

The young mother would often help Linda with weddings. While her husband was the Chaplain's Assistant at Walter Reed Army Hospital she worked for the Chaplain's office and often had three to four weddings to work every weekend. She would always try and make it very special for these soldiers. "It was their only wedding" she said. She would use things from the big weddings for the smaller weddings, making it special for those soldiers and brides who were less fortunate. She wanted them to have wonderful memories.

Lois

Lois and Arnold married on January 28, 1956. Six months later Arnold joined the U.S. Air Force on July 3, 1956. While he was in basic training, Lois went home to be with her family because she was expecting her first child. Arnold was then stationed in California. Soon after Lois was expecting her second child. Arnold did not see either of his children until they were six to eight months old.

During his career he was stationed all over the world. He had tours of duty literally across the world in Thailand and Iceland. Lois could only communicate to her husband by mail. She recalls one day being frightened by seeing the mailman accompanied by two Federal Bureau of Investigations (FBI) agents come to her door. They assured her they were only there to make sure the funds from her husband were in the envelope and correct. You see, someone had been stealing money from the envelopes that were being sent home to families from the soldiers. Arnold always sent his pay by a money order.

Lois reflects on being a wife, mother, referee, tutor, mechanic and a TV repairwoman. She remembers a time when the TV went on the blink. Back then the TV's had tubes you could replace. She had a book at home that Arnold had bought with all the tubes names and substitutions so she could have it just in case. She went into the repair shop on base to get a tube. Getting frustrated because every tube she asked for did not work or the repair shop did not have. Finally, she just picked one, paid for it and went home and prayed it would work. She felt great pride in this accomplishment. It worked!

Lois received a lot of support from her church family and friends. There were nights when she cried and felt alone. She would make sure the kids did not see her. They would know when she was having a bad day because she missed Arnold and was dealing with the everyday struggles. Her faith got her through each day. She is thankful that her husband came home safely after each assignment away from home.

Arnold retired from the Air Force in 1977.

Sarah

Sarah is 21 years old and is engaged to marry her high school sweetheart, Ryan, a U.S. Marine. Her fiancé, Ryan, is serving in

Operation Iraqi Freedom as a helicopter mechanic. He left for Iraq in February 2004. Hope is that he will return home in September. Sarah hears from him about every one to two weeks. When Ryan calls home, he often waits in line at the communications center for up to three hours to use the phone. She also communicates with Ryan by email.

Sarah keeps busy by going to school and working as a waitress. She waitresses at night to keep herself busy. After high school they separated. Ryan joined the Marines and while at boot camp missed Sarah. The separation proved to be too much and they got back together.

Sarah has never experienced military life before but since 9-11 she realizes that alot of things were going to come about; it was going to be a hard ride. She didn't know what to expect. But she supported Ryan's decision. They write letters. Sarah sends care packages with DVD's, CD's, letters, candy and books.

Sarah has the support of Ryan's mother. Ryan's mom encourages her with cards and calls to check on her and is always there if Sarah just needs to talk. Sarah never realized the reality of war. She had her own life and never thought about the events going on in the world.

Our military makes her proud now. She tries to keep busy and not think about bad things that could happen. She counts the days now when he is to come home instead of how many days it has been since he left. She comforts herself by wearing his clothes. She sleeps in his t-shirts. Sometimes she will wear his cologne to smell his scent. She will often go into his room at his house and lay on his bed where his sheets have not been changed since he left. His razor still sits on the bathroom sink on the left side. Sarah is anxiously waiting for Ryan's return. Sarah told me of a time when she was unable to encourage a friend whose husband was deployed. She did not understand and she felt helpless. Now experiencing it she understands all to well what feelings her friend went through.

Proclamation by the President of the United States

Whereas the service rendered the United States by the American mother is the greatest source of the Country's strength and inspiration; and "Whereas we honor ourselves and the mothers of America when we revere and give emphasis to the home as the fountainhead of the State; and "Whereas the American mother is doing so much for the home and for the moral and spiritual uplift of the people of the United States and hence so much for good government and humanity; and "Whereas the American Gold Star Mothers suffered the supreme sacrifice of motherhood in the loss of their sons and daughters in World Wars" and "Whereas the said Public Resolution 12 provides:
"That the President of the United States is hereby authorized and requested to issue a proclamation calling upon the Government officials to display the United States flag on all Government buildings, and the people of the United States to display the flag and to hold appropriate meetings in their homes, churches, or other suitable places, on the last Sunday in September, as public expression of the love, sorrow and reverence of the people of the United States for the American Gold Star Mothers."

"Sec. 2. That the last Sunday in September shall hereafter be designated and known as "Gold Star Mother's Day," and it shall be the duty of the President to request its observance as provided for in this resolution." (www.goldstarmom.com)

Claire

Claire never met her Uncle Sonny but feels like she has known him all her life. Sonny was killed in action during WWII on February 25, 1945. As I sat with Claire amongst all the photos and newspaper articles that were handed down to her from her mother after she died, I got to know Sonny. I saw the love and respect she had for him and wanted so desperately to know him personally. The memorabilia of his life is all she has.

Sonny lived most of his life in his home town of Fall River, Massachusetts with his mother and sisters; he was the man of the house. He often traveled to Canada to visit with his father. He was devoted to his parents and sisters and was very protective of his family.

—*Herald News Photo*

HONOR MEMORY OF PFC CHASSE: Flag is presented to St. Vincent's Home by relatives of the late PFC Armand J. Chasse, who was killed in action in Germany on Feb. 25, 1945, in Veterans Day Ceremony, yesterday. Left to right are his sister, Mrs. Adrien Beauregard, nieces Claire and Jacqueline, his mother, Mrs. Armand Chasse, and Rev. John E. Boyd who received flag on behalf of the Home.

Her mother - Sonny's sister - never talked much about him after his death because it was too painful. But she had her memories of her brother to keep her warm. Her grandmother - Sonny's mother - would tell funny stories of Sonny. You knew when to begin and when to end the conversation about Uncle Sonny. Sonny joined the Army on May 13, 1943. He was respected by all his associates and devotion to duty. Sonny was 26 when he was killed while occupying a building in a town which his platoon had just taken from the enemy east of the Roer River and in the vicinity of Duren, Germany. He was killed by a fragment of the shell and was buried in an American Cemetery **somewhere** in Belgium. His body was not brought home until two years after his death.

WAR DEPARTMENT
THE ADJUTANT GENERAL'S OFFICE
RECORDS ADMINISTRATION CENTER
4300 GOODFELLOW BOULEVARD
ST. LOUIS 20, MISSOURI

IN REPLY
REFER TO:
AGRS-DC 201 Chasse, Armand J.
(15 Oct 45)

1 July 1946.

Mrs. Clara M. Chasse
363 Sunset Hill
Fall River, Massachusetts.,

Dear Mrs. Chasse;

Reference is made to your letter addressed to The Adjutant General, Washington 25, D. C., requesting additional information regarding the death of your son.

Additional information has now been received which confirms the previous report of the death of your son, Private First Class Armand J. Chasse, Army serial number 31 356 385, Infantry, and shows that he received severe injuries on 25 February 1945 near Oberzier, Germany when the building which he was occupying was struck by a projectile from a three inch gun. He was evacuated to the 44th Evacuation Hospital at Brand, Germany where every possible medical aid was administered in an effort to save his life but death occurred that same day as the result of those injuries. I regret that no further details were given.

At the time of your son's death he was serving a member of Troop B, 24th Cavalry Reconnaissance Squadron, Mechanized, which was assigned to the First United States Army.

The Quartermaster General of the Army, Washington 25, D. C., has jurisdiction over matters pertaining to the burial of our military personnel who die overseas. A copy of your letter has accordingly been forwarded to that officer for necessary action.

Permit me to extend my sympathy in the loss you have sustained.

Sincerely yours,

Charles D. Carle

CHARLES D. CARLE
Colonel, AGD
Commanding

Claire grew up hearing many funny stories about him. She has felt angry at times but mostly sad because he was taken from her family. She felt they really needed him. Claire says, "I often wonder what our lives would have been like with him around to love and guide us." In just 26 years he gave his family more love and warm wonderful memories than most parents receive from their children in a lifetime. He helped keep his family in line. Sonny is Claire's hero and a role model of what it means to be a man. He was very proud to be a soldier and serve his country. Claire promised to her mother and grandmother that she would cherish his memory and care for his belongings.

When I sat with Claire she gave me two letters that were written in French in 1946. Until recently, the letters had never been translated. I told Claire that I would try and find someone to translate them for her. After a two month search, I found someone, and on June 4, 2004 I met Robert Blanche. He and his wife are French. I sat with Mr. Blanche in the lobby of the dentists office as he read these letters dated back 60 years. I was in awe as he spoke the language of friends writing to Sonny's mother from Germany in English. I listened as he read and noticed tears welling up in his eyes. I spoke to him about WWII. He told me how he had walked on the beaches of Normandy and you just cannot explain the feeling. He was a very kind and gentle man who turned a woman's feelings of emptiness from not knowing what the letters said into great and utter joy.

Ce 19-9-1946.

Chers Monsieur et Madame Chassé

Depuis bien longtemps nous n'avons plus reçu de vos nouvelles, nous attendions et ne recevant rien, nous nous décidons à vous écrire.

N'auriez-pas reçu notre dernière lettre, dans laquelle je vous envoyai les pellicules des photos du cimetière; j'espère pourtant qu'elles vous sont parvenues, quand à nous, nous n'avons jamais reçu les photos que vous nous annonciez peut-être ont elles été égarées. Dimanche 15 septembre par une belle journée il y a eu au cimetière de Henrichapelle une cérémonie religieuse où il y avait plus de 2,000 personnes, nous y sommes allés, on a célébré la messe dans la Chapelle, il y avait de hautes personnalités, on a prononcé plusieurs discours, qui rappelaient la libération et le courage des soldats alliés les liens qui unissent notre pays au notre. La foule observe une minute de silence un délégué américain remercie

et on joue l'hymne américain et
la Brabançonne c'est-à-dire notre chant
national; le prêtre alors bénit les
tombes fleuries et la cérémonie prend
fin. Nous espérons bien y aller encore
quelques fois avant l'hiver.
Je ne voulais pas laisser passer cette
cérémonie sans vous écrire, d'autant
plus que le mois de septembre nous
rappelle notre libération ce jour qui
ne s'effacera jamais de notre mémoire
J'espère que ma lettre ira vous trouver
en bonne santé ainsi que notre
famille, et nous espérons recevoir
de vos nouvelles bientôt. Je vous prie
de recevoir chers Monsieur et Madame
Chassé les meilleures pensées de
vos amis de Belgique.

François Lassotte Talla
Wégimont Micheroux
Province de Liège Belgique

Le 15-12-1946.

Cher Monsieur et Madame Chassé,

Je réponds à votre lettre qui nous à fait grand plaisir, merci beaucoup pour vos belles photos, vous êtes tous très bien, et vos petites filles sont charmantes. Depuis que je vous avais écrit Jenny est allée encore à Henrichapelle en voiture avec les parents de son fiancé. Il y a quelques semaines une dame américaine est venue en Belgique afin de visiter le cimetière où son fils est enterré elle à séjourné deux mois ici à un demi heure de chez nous elle à paraît-il promis de revenir l'année prochaine. si vous aussi vous pouviez venir, quelle consolation ce serait pour nous. Nous avons eu un très bon mois de novembre de la pluie en décembre, et au moment où je vous écris le temps s'est mis à la gelée et il fait très froid un vrai temps de Noël. La vie ici n'est pas encore normale, depuis bientôt 7 ans nous ne sommes pas encore libres et surtout pour nous fermiers, nous connaissons encore certaines contraintes que nous avions pendant l'occupation ennemie, alors que l'on espérait tant après la libération, et il paraît que l'on est encore mieux que dans beaucoup de pays. Espérons que cela changera avec l'année nouvelle. Je vous souhaite à toute la famille une très bonne fête de Noël et de nouvel An, que l'année qui va commencer vous apporte la santé, et la réalisation de vos plus chers désirs.

Un grand bonjour à vos aimables petites filles et pour vous tous nos meilleures amitiés de toute la famille

F. Lassotte - Jalla
Wégimont Micheroux
Province de Liège
Belgique.

Marie

Letter 1
This 19th day of September 1946

Dear Mr. And Mrs. Chasse,
It's been along time we didn't have any news. We are waiting and getting nothing. We have decided to write to you. Did you get our last letter in which I send you some picture of a cemetery? I hope you get them but for us we never had any picture, which you say you were going to send to us. Maybe they have been lost. Sunday, Sept. 15 it's a beautiful day and the cemetery of Henry Chappell where there was a religious ceremony where there were more than 2000 people. We get there and we celebrated a mass in the chapel where there were very high personalities (very high people), which they pronounced several speech. Were talking about the liberation and the bravery of the allied American soldier and the tie which between our country and the US. The crowd observed a minute of silence and an American delegate gives thanks to everybody and we played American and the Drubanconne, which is our national anthem. The priest blessed all the grave and the ceremony finished. We hope to go again several times before the winter. I did not want to let go this occasion without writing to you. As especially this month of September brings us back memories of our liberation. It is a day we will never forget. I hope we find you in good health and your family. We hope to receive some of your news soon. Please dear Mr. And Mrs. Chasse our best wishes for you from your friend from Belgium.

Letter 2
This 15th day of December

Dear Mr. and Mrs. Chasse,
I answered to your letter, which bringeth big pleasure to read. Thank you very much for the beautiful picture, you all look beautiful and your little girl very charming. Since I wrote to you Jenny went to the cemetery one more time the cemetery with a car with the parents of a fiancée. Several weeks ago an American lady came to Belgium to visit the cemetery where her son is buried. She stayed here two months about a ½ hour from where we live. She going to come back next year. If you also could come what a consolation it will be for you. We have a very good month of Nov. The rain in Dec. At the moment where I write to you the weather is freezing. It is very cold. It's a real Christmas weather. Life here is not yet normal. It's almost seven years and we not free yet. Especially for us who are farmers we still have some (unclear). The (unclear) during the German occupation. We were hoping so much after the liberation and (unclear) with the other country it's much better than where we are. We hope that will change with the next year. We wish you that to your family a very nice Christmas and a happy New Year and we hope New Year will start to bring you good health and the realization of your best wishes. A big hello to your charming little girl and for you all our best of friendship from all the family.

Sonny's mother, Clara, joined the Gold Star Mothers chapter in Fall River, MA. To this day Claire does not know if her grandmother joined right away or 10 years later. Claire remembers at eight years old seeing her grandmother in her Gold Star Mothers uniform. She would attend the parades and watch her grandmother walk with the women of the Gold Star Mothers chapter. The chapter would often meet and always supported each other. Claire chuckles as she remembers going to a few meetings with her grandmother and hearing women speaking in French, Portuguese and Italian.

The Gold Star Mothers is a group of women who had lost a son in WWI. Gold Star Mothers is a nondenominational, non-profit, non-political national organization incorporated under the laws of the District of Columbia on January 5, 1929 by a group of twenty-five mothers living in Washington D.C. Soon many small groups of Gold Star Mothers began under local and state charters. During the 1941 National Convention, the membership to Gold Star Mothers was opened to mothers who had lost a son or daughter in WWII and again opened after the Korean Conflict (www.goldstarmoms.com).

On June 12th, 1984 the Ninety-Eighth Congress of the United

States granted the American Gold Star Mothers, Inc. a charter. Almost all chapters of American Gold Star Mothers throughout the United States give countless hours of volunteer service, serving in hospitals for veterans and to their families. Claire remembers the pain in her mother's eyes as she tried to deal with her brother's death. Claire feels Sonny's mom or sister never really accepted his death and never blamed anyone for his death. He wanted to go and serve his country. Yes, he wanted to be home but he knew he had a job to do and gave his life for a good cause.

Claire is eager to keep Uncle Sonny's memory alive. By telling his story she is able to do just that.

Katy

Katy and Greg have been married for almost 34 years. They have a son, Kyle. Her husband, Greg served in the U.S. Air Force as an F15 pilot in the Persian Gulf War. Katy had a trememdous amount of support while separated from her husband. One thing that really impacted Katy was the support of people she knew that would help her out while her soldier was away. This community we live in is very supportive of our military. You make a lot of acquaintenances along the way but very few friends. She continues to keep in touch with those she had made lasting friendships with including friends overseas. The relationships that you have are very intense. You get to know each other well and what your husband does in the military.

Katy and Greg taught their son Kyle, that no matter what adversities come along in life you just say okay you need to move on. Greg made tapes for his son that told him nightly bedtime stories. He would take your regular bedtime story and add a little twist. Kyle's friends would often ask if they could come over to hear his dad's stories. Katy feels the letters, phone calls and tapes helped Kyle deal with the separation.

Katy remembers a time while living in Arizona when Kyle was a baby. Katy was hosting a belated Thanksgiving dinner for the entire squadron of 300 people on base. Her mother died that morning and Katy was notified when the dinner was just beginning. Her husband told her, "You are just going to have to get through it." It wasn't that her husband did not care but when you are married to a soldier you just can't pack up and go when you want to. Greg's commander was notified and supported her as she struggled to get through those three hours and then return home.

Katy says people don't go into the military now like they did back in the day. People go in the military now for school. The difference that she says as to why people go into the military nowadays has a great deal of impact on their adaptation to it.

Katy missed the military initially upon her husband retiring. But she says you quickly adjust. As a working spouse she could never depend on her retirement because she was always moving. She does not miss the moving. It has been 13 years since Greg has retired. After three years goes by she feels like it's time to paint. You know you are going to move. The whole mindset is you are only here for a short time.

Greg was known to be writing letters all the time. Katy has all her letters from Greg. She also has the letters from her mom that her dad wrote while he was in WWII. She has a whole box of memories that she will give to her son to keep the memories alive.

Mary

Mary and her husband Frank have been married for 14 years. Frank has served in the United States Navy for 15 years. Eight days after they were married in 1990, he was sent to war during Operation DESERT SHIELD/DESERT STORM. Mary remembers watching the news way too much and worried herself sick. Listening to the radio stations and watching the news just fed her fear. Prior to the start of the Persian Gulf War, there had been an accident involving one of the helicopters from the flight deck her sailor worked on. Mary was racked with fear. Then she got the call that her sailor was OK, but the crash had claimed the lives of the pilots and the helicopter had crashed into the water, not the ship.

Mary communicated mostly by letter with her sailor. She would get letters maybe twice a week and a phone call once a month depending on when he was in port.

She has become quite the pack rat, keeping all of his letters even those letters from before they were married. She has pictures of places he has visited, newspaper clippings, and newsletters from family support groups.

Mary stayed up late alot, mostly due to sleeplessness dealing with "Empty Bed" syndrome. It was difficult to go to bed without her husband by her side.

She spent time with friends, stayed busy with work, and focused on the homecoming date. Getting involved with the family support group and meetings was a great way to form relationships with others in the same boat. There is a lot to learn from other families that have experiences with deployments. To stay comforted and close to him, Mary would wear his t-shirt at night with his cologne sprayed on it. She slept with a giant teddy bear he had given her.

Already an independent person, and because she had to be, Mary's life was shaping. Her strengths increased along with her faith in God. Her faith early on was only a fraction of what it is now, she prayed all the time.

Growing up she was an only child and her mom worked, so she learned to do just about everything for herself. Her family moved many times as she grew up. She sometimes felt like God was preparing her to be a military wife. As the wife of a deployed Navy man, she had to learn to ask for help, that asking for help was not a sign of weakness, but a way of gaining strength. It gave purpose to the struggles she grew up with and taught her to be helpful instead of feeling helpless.

While doing her student teaching, Operation Desert Storm was gearing up. Her teachers were very supportive and always asked about her Navy man. She had friends that were very loving and tried to be supportive.

No one really understands until they have been personally affected by war and deployed loved ones. There is no real way that a civilian who has never known a person on deployment or at war could ever fully understand the emotional, physical, and mental challenges we are faced with each day. There is no true moment of peace, whether deployed or at home because at any moment the phone could ring, the orders could change and things are on the move again.

Mary would pass on these words to encourage other military wives. "Find your inner strength." Learn to ask for help, find God and trust Him. Don't be discouraged. Your serviceman needs you, loves you, and will come home soon. If things aren't going well, communicate with him, even when it hurts. Don't be afraid to ask for help. Life does not come with an owner's manual.

Combat loneliness by getting involved, volunteering, working, and just getting out of the house. When you focus on others the load always seems lighter. If you have children, love them, read to them, take them out and play. They miss daddy too.

Most importantly, take care of yourself. Pamper yourself once in a while. When you look in a mirror, know are loved and that there are many others going through what you are going through. Remember, what doesn't kill you will only make you stronger. One step at a time. One month; one week; one day; one hour; one minute; one second at a time until he is home. Celebrate all things that are cause for joy, no matter how small.

Moms support troops and each other

When dark thoughts about her son's safety start to interrupt Cheryl Gray's day, she knows there is a person she can turn to who understands exactly what she's going through.

That is Debbie Kepler, whose son also is stationed in the Middle East.

Leslie Evans of Genoa stopped reading newspapers and listening to newscasts even though her husband owns two radio stations.

Sally Diamond Wiley of Gardnerville found herself in Wal-Mart spending $192 — "a mother thing" — buying everything from Easter candy to bug spray for her then-36-year-old son Sean stationed in Baghdad, even though he was within commuting distance to Burger King and the military store.

See **GARDNER** on 2C

SHEILA GARDNER

Williams — Provided by family
Diamond — Provided by family
Birchill — Provided by family
Kepler — Provided by family
Evans — Provided by family

STICKING TOGETHER: Cheryl Gray, from left, Sally Diamond, Carol Birchill, Debbie Kepler and Leslie Evans pose Monday in front of Piñon Hills Elementary School, where Kepler is a teacher.

Lisa J. Tolda/Reno Gazette-Journal

The service flag is an official banner authorized by the Department of Defense for display by families who have members serving in the Armed Forces during any period of war or hostilities the United States may be engaged in for the duration of such hostilities.

The service flag (also called the blue star flag) was designed and patented by World War I Army Captain Robert L. Queissner of the 5th Ohio Infantry who had two sons serving on the front line. The flag quickly became the unofficial symbol of a child in service. President Wilson became part of this history when in 1918 he approved a suggestion made by the Women's Committee of the Council of National Defenses that mothers who had lost a child serving in the war to wear a gold gilt star on the traditional black mourning arm band.

The history of the service flag is as patriotic and touching as the symbolism each star represents to the families that display them. The color of the stars is also symbolic in that the blue star represents hope and pride and the gold star represents sacrifice to the cause of liberty and freedom. The Service flag is an indoor flag and should be flown facing out from the front window of the home or organization. If a gold star is added to the Service flag, it should take the position of honor and be placed over the blue star that is positioned closest to the staff.

During World War II, the practice of displaying the Service flag became much more widespread. In 1942, the Blue Star Mothers of America was founded as a veteran service organization and was part of a movement to provide care packages to military members serving overseas and also provide assistance to families who encountered hardships as a result of their son or husband serving during the war.

Virtually every home and organization displayed banners to indicate the number of members of the family or organization serving in the Armed Forces, and again, covered those blue stars with a gold star to represent each member that died. Displaying the Service flag recognizes and honors the service member as well as the family that displays the flag. (Copyright 2001, ServiceFlags.com, Inc., 1982 Highway 50 East, Carson City, Nevada 89701. (775) 841-6227).

Cheryl

Cheryl's son, Matthew, is 19 years old. He joined the Army in 2003 during his senior year of high school under the Delayed Entry Program. He left for basic training in July after graduation from high school. He is now serving in Iraq as an Intelligence Analyst. Matthew is looking forward to becoming a police officer after his time in the military.

Matt is currently stationed in Tikrit, Iraq. He escorts Iraqi workers around the grounds. As a mom, Cheryl thinks having her son experience different cultures and interaction with others is a great experience for him. Cheryl recalls a story about Matt. One day he was carrying around a big bag of candy and offered the Iraqis some. They grabbed the whole bag and stuffed their pockets.

Cheryl sends her son care packages at least once a week and fills it with all kinds of fun things to eat. He is also getting care packages from friends and other family members. He loves getting his care packages and can't wait to see what surprises are in there. He also enjoys getting mail and emails from home. A local grade school in his hometown sent Matt 100 postcards mailed separately. He got a big kick out of that and answers every single child with a letter.

Cheryl feels very fortunate to be able to communicate with her son through email. She gets to email Matt about every other day. He is also able to call once a week. She still sends him letters in the mail.

Just like all of us connected to a military soldier, Cheryl has to cope with her son being away at war. Being a single mom it has been extremely hard. When Matt left for basic training she cried constantly. One month prior to his leaving she gave him a graduation party. At that party, a big collage of pictures from birth to age ten was made for him and set up in their home on the fireplace. It gave her great comfort to look at those pictures of him growing up and seeing what a wonderful young man he had grown up to be. She would cry some more but would tell herself constantly that if he wasn't away in the Army he would be away at college and that all this is a part of life.

Cheryl has a picture of Matt with her friends' grandkids. The kids are crazy about soldiers in uniform. Matt put on his uniform and went to visit them at their home. He had two American flags that he gave them. They were so proud and Matt seemed bigger than life to them.

Cheryl doesn't think Matt has missed out on much. She looks at this as a chapter in his life and this is where he is right now. He really wants to see the world right now and this is a part of his journey. While he is away, he is often happy to hear when told a new store or restaurant has opened in their small town.

Matt has two best friends who are also in the military. One of them is in Iraq and the other one in Germany. They communicate by email frequently. This helps to keep them close. Cheryl commented that one of his friends says, "This is like we are all hanging out together still."

Cheryl and one of her son's best friends mother have become very close. They started out just comforting one another and crying on each other's shoulders. They began talking about forming a support group for other mother's whose sons are in the military. Talk has become reality; there are now six mothers who have joined the group and they are working on becoming Nevada's first chapter of the Blue Star Mothers.

Cheryl is very proud of America. She is a very emotional person and gets choked up when she hears a patriotic song. She is very proud that her son is out there fighting for our country and our freedom. She says, "Where would our country be without our military fighting for what we stand for?"

Her heart goes out to families who have lost a loved one fighting for our country. She always hears the same thing from every wife and mother, "they were doing what they wanted to do and they would willingly give their life for their country." Cheryl keeps the faith and continues to let our soldiers know she supports them 100%. Our soldiers need to be told all the time how proud we are of them and how much we are behind them.

Cheryl gets through the separation by crying when she needs too. She has faith in God and knows he will take care of her son. She feels her biggest obstacle to deal with is that she misses him very much and wishes he were closer to home but she continues to tell herself that he is doing what he wants to do and she is extremely proud of him and the direction he has chosen and supports him all the way.

Sally

Sally's son, Sean, served in Operation Iraqi Freedom with the 94th Engineering Combat Support Group from January thru September 2003. Sean had been in the reserves for many years and then decided to leave his reserve unit and go active duty again. Sean has an identical twin, Michael, and a younger brother Jason.

Sean's brother, Michael, was sick with Non-Hodgkin's Lymphoma and was receiving bone marrow treatments. Before Sean left for Germany he donated bone marrow to his brother. Michael was living in Washington at the time so Sean flew from the Bay area to Seattle to prepare for the transplant. Sally remembers going back and forth to Seattle to help Michael with his family. She also had friends Lucy and Paul, whose wedding Sally was in 37 years ago, and also are godparents to her youngest son, Jason. Two weeks after Sean's bone marrow transplant for Michael, Sally donated a kidney to her friend, Paul. She is so amazed at life's events. Had it not been for Michael's cancer, she would not have know how bad her friend Paul was or that she could have even been a donor.

Sally had to deal with the thought of losing a child. Sean saved Michael's life and she extended her friend's life. Sally says, "Dreadful events happen and yet the most wonderful events can happen as a result." Sally would look back on this experience to get her through her son Sean's departure for war. It was a reminder of how wonderful life can be and a reminder that there would be great things happening to someone else because of what Sean was doing.

All of Sally's love for her son could not keep him out of harm's way. Even believing that life is in God's hands-not-ours, and keeping positive thoughts could not take away the agony that her son is going to war. She thought Sean giving his brother a chance to live was enough, "wasn't it?" she asks.

"Did the Combat Support Group not know that his brother needed him as much as they did?" Yes, she was proud of what he was doing for his country. These were all the emotions Sally was dealing with. Sally was not able to talk with her son until he returned to Germany nine months later.

As the war began, she was glued to the TV, her hand glued to the remote and switching from channel to channel. She would even write down which reporter with each major news channel was embedded with the infantry group that her son was traveling with.

Sean's wife was her connection to her son. They were in Germany. She was able to provide Sally with updates from her son. His family was able to see him on video conference calls and was able to tell Sally how her son looked.

Sean turned 36 years old in Kuwait. Soon after his arrival in Baghdad Sean was able to provide his mom with an address so she could send him care packages and mail directly.

She remembers going into a Rite Aid store, walking up and down the aisles, silently crying and picking up every item she thought would make him okay. She spent $192.00, but then ended up taking half of it back. As she found out later, large packages take longer to get to the soldier. She also found out that he was near a PX store and Burger King, making it a little more convenient for him to purchase what he needed.

Whenever Sally watched the news and saw that a soldier has been killed or wounded, her heart seemed to stop. When she found out it was not her son, she cried with happiness at him being spared but at the same time her heart went out to the families that did suffer a loss.

She experienced all kinds of emotions, both positive and negative. She spent a lot of time worrying and praying "when will it ever end? Was it right to be there?" knowing in her heart it was right. Thinking what would happen to his wife and children if something happened to him. How could she make it better for them? But she knew that it was not her place but God's to do so.

She was so proud of Sean and what he was doing and not wanting him there. She wanted him to still be the warm and loving child playing outside in the dirt with his GI Joe's and trucks with his brothers. He has grown into a man serving his country.

"There does not seem to be any middle ground, a child is a child in his mother's mind, no matter what their age. You admire them as adults yet still yearn to protect them; it is a feeling that is magnified when they are in harm's way."

Sally's faith is what got her through it. Her family, friends, organizations that provide support to the troops helped. She is especially greatful for the Blue Star Mother's Group in the area.

Sean is back home in Germany now and not sure when he will be deployed again. Sally is hoping it will not but realizes that she could experience it all again. Sally says he and his fellow soldiers are the best in the world, "God bless them all for their sacrifices on our behalf. Thank God for the gift of faith."

Sally has pictures of all three of her sons and their families. She has placed them where she can see them all the time. Sean is in his Army fatigues with his wife and children. His brothers along with their mom, aunts, and uncles. The images of her sons give her great strength and comfort.

The Army experience is of great benefit to Sean and his family. The children are learning German in school. Being able to travel and meeting new people is such a great opportunity. She talks with Sean every week which brings her great joy and comfort. When she calls she always says, "Hi, Sean, it's your mom." He knows it is her and does not correct her by saying he knows. She feels he senses the great pride she feels for his service to his country and it brings a sense of well being to her and serves as a reminder that he is indeed a son, husband, father, and soldier.

Seeing and hearing any acts of patriotism make Sally cry happy tears. "I am so proud to be an American," she says. Her husband will automatically pull out his handkerchief from his back pocket and hand it to her when they hear the Star Spangled Banner or America, the Beautiful. When she sees a soldier currently serving or a veteran, she shakes their hand and thanks them for their service and for helping to make the world a safer place to live in."

Sally would offer these words to anyone who has a family member in the military, "Have faith in God; pray often and stay positive. Be strong when they need you; laugh when they laugh. Keep the packages, letters, pictures, emails going. Praise them;

thank them for their valor, for their duty to God and country. Remind them that loved ones are rooting for them as well as praying for them. They are never alone!"

Leslie

Leslie has family background of military service. Her father served in the Navy during WWII, an uncle took part in the Normandy invasion, and her brother served in Vietnam. (Carson & Douglas Reno Gazette-Journal). Leslie's son Henry is 20 years old. He has been in the military for eleven months. He knew as a small child that he wanted to serve his country first and then get an education.

Since the time that her children understood, it was instilled in them that their priorities are God, country, and family.

September 11, 2002 had a big effect on Henry's decision to join the military. Henry joined the U.S. Army on July 9th 2003. He is very happy to serve his country and his parents could never be more proud of him. Leslie recalls many fond memories over the past eleven months of her son's service. The day his grandmother pinned on his infantry cord was very special. Henry's grandpa had died during his senior year in high school. Henry was very close to his grandpa and affected deeply by his death. When Henry entered the Army he carried a picture of his grandparents in his pocket all the time. Through all of his trials he says he could feel his grandfather's presence. He knew without a doubt that God was watching over him but also believed his grandpa was right there in spirit. Leslie says as she stood and watched Henry's grandma pin his infantry cord, she knew that his grandpa was smiling down on all of them. Henry communicates by phone as often as he can. Leslie gets her support by her very close family and her belief in Jesus Christ. Her family's faith in God is first and foremost. Love of her country and the pride in her son for his bravery and strength of character.

Leslie looks forward to when she can speak to her son. Leslie feels that her son has missed out on the last years of father son bonding. She knows that those memories they have made together will stay with them the rest of their lives. Tears of pride always fill

Leslie's eyes when she sees an American soldier.

Leslie's words of encouragement that she would offer another mother or spouse of a soldier would be "steer clear of the national news. Be proud of your spouses, children and tell them that too. Pray." I asked Leslie how do you do it? She says, "You just do it. We know that Henry is in God's hands. Our belief in Jesus Christ and our pride in our dear son get us through it all." One of Leslie's goals as a Blue Star Mother is to revive support for the troops. "It's of the utmost importance to spread the word that our sons and daughters are fighting a just war." (Carson & Douglas Reno Gazette-Journal).

Debbie

Debbie's son, Derrick, left for boot camp on June 17th 2003. Derrick wants to become a police officer and knew by joining the U.S. Marines he would receive good training. After graduating from high school on a Friday, he left for boot camp on Sunday. He is a Marine and currently deployed to Iraq. He has been in Iraq since February 2004. Currently in the city of Ramadi, Derrick has already experienced the horror of war. On April 6, the city was attacked and his battalion lost 12 Marines. Two of those soldiers were good friends of his. "I miss him and worry about him all the time," she says.

When her son's battalion was attacked in April she had no contact with him. She read the news, watched the news every day, praying that Casualty Affairs would not come to her door to tell her that her son had been killed. She wore his class ring on a chain around her neck so he would be close to her heart.

Debbie knows his experience is far more than she could ever imagine he would experience in life. As a mom, it was the hardest thing she had to go through seeing her son lose two of his friends. When your children are little and get hurt you kiss their boo-boos. When their hearts are broken for the first time, you are there to comfort them and tell them it is part of growing up and they will be alright. But Debbie is not able to do that now. It is very hard for her. Debbie says, "I just take it one day at a time. I don't watch the news anymore. I pray alot and have alot of faith in God and know he has a plan for Derrick's life and mine." She knows this has been an amazing experience for him. He appreciates his country and freedoms we have even more. Derrick has had to grow up real fast. Derrick has just started emailing home within the past month. He is usually able to call once a week but it depends on how things are going on any given day.

Debbie has been married for 20 years. Her husband is her rock. He helps her when there doesn't seem to be a bright side to anything. He helps her see the good side.

Debbie is very proud to be an American and appreciates all the great things we have every day that we take for granted, like our freedom. She would offer these words of encouragement. "Pray a lot; have faith; take it one day at a time; focus on the here and now. Don't think about the "what if's." Go to counseling if that helps. Get into a support group or just talk to other people who are dealing with the same thing."

Mrs. Smith

Mrs. Smith is the mother of two sons both of whom served in the Persian Gulf War at the same time. Elliot is the youngest and decided he wanted to go into the Marines at the end of high school. One day he walked into the kitchen home and said he had to go to see a recruiter and then walked in one night and said he had joined the Marines. He left during the summer when the recruiter came and picked him up to go to Parris Island, South Carolina. Mom had mixed emotions about him going because she really wanted him to go to college. He was 18 and chose to join the Marines rather than go to Virginia State University. He joined the Marines in 1988. He went to the Gulf War in 1990.

The Christmas of 1990 was not good for her. She put up a small tree. Elliot was serving in Okinawa and called his family to say he was leaving to serve in the Gulf War.

The plane was boarding soldiers by last name alphabetically. When they got to the S's the first plane was full. His family did not hear from him for a few weeks.

The oldest son, Phillip, was in the Air Force Reserves. He was called off his job to go active duty and when he got to Langley Air Force Base he found out that he was going to the Gulf War. He came home and said he had to go to war! He went right away.

Phillip was in the air the night that the war started. Phillip was the first to get there and Eliot came about two weeks later. While Phillip was there he tried to find his brother and after a few weeks found out his brother was there but were not able to talk with each other.

Mrs. Smith did not have to deal with each son differently and responded to each son in the same way. She would send them care packages. The hardest time was dealing with both her sons gone and waiting to hear from them. She received her support from her church, family and coworkers.

Neither son showed any fear; they were calm and knew what they had to do and served their country. They have the strength and were brought up in a christian home. They knew how to cope. Elliot came back the first weekend in May and Philip came back a few weeks earlier.

Mrs. Smith is a retired schoolteacher. She taught third grade and recalls a time when it was her birthday while her sons were at war. Someone came to her classroom door knocking and asked her to step outside. Everyone on her hall sang "Happy Birthday" to her and gave her a beautiful card.

She speaks of a minister who would bring his granddaughter to school every day and would walk by her classroom. The young girl was not even in her class. To this day Mrs. Smith does not know who cared enough to tell him her two sons were at war. Once he found out he would stop by daily and tell her they are going to be alright, "I'm praying for them." Everyday!" "It meant so much to me", she said. He encouraged her every day. Her sons were on her mind daily and she prayed for them. She would send care packages to them. She says to make sure you have good support. It is what will carry you. Home, church, family, and coworkers. If not available, seek out your support groups within the unit.

Her son Elliot does not talk much about the war anymore except on occasion when he recalls how hot the weather was. Upon returning from the war, Phillip went back to the reserve unit he served in and his job.

Mrs. Smith says both her boys had adjusted well with being home. She is very proud of her sons and they were very proud to serve. More than fear, it became very interesting for them.

This war has brought back memories of previous wars. Her heart still goes out to those who have lost their soldiers. She has felt more sadness for this war than when her sons served in the Gulf War. So many more soldiers' lives are being lost.

She showed me a photo from the local newspaper from 1991 featuring her sons and she says it was a "happy day having both of them back" their father says, "I guess you couldn't do anything better than serving your country."

Both brothers are proud to have served their country and have families of their own with beautiful children.

Kelly

Kelly and her husband, Keith, have been married for 14 years. They were married when Keith knew he was leaving to serve in Desert Storm in 1990. He wanted her to be taken care of if something should happen. She remembers when the first bombings began. She was playing basketball and stopped immediately when she heard the announcement that the war had begun. She immediately went home and turned on the TV and watched it all night crying, and wondering what we had gotten ourselves into. Being military herself, she knew she had to be strong because she worked a lot with the orderly room and took care of the phone calls for the spouses left behind.

Keith served for eight months and then was forced to come home due to an injury. He was diving into a bunker one night and tore the ligaments in his knee. While he was away, Kelly wrote letters every day, sometimes two and three times a day. She always sent him cards telling him how much she loved him and missed him. She did have an opportunity to fax messages but there was no email. It was difficult for her to cope because she had no family that was local. The Air Force was her family.

She frequently relied on long distance phone calls from her parents and brother. She tried to stay busy and stay away from the news on TV. Her brother told her something that will always stay with her forever, "Kelly, just look at this as a football game and we are sitting in the stands, once the American people see how strategic our bombs and how talented our pilots are, the crowd will change their ways, people are going to be excited at our accomplishments."

He was right, Kelly says. He was right because he was a United States Marine and that is what she needed to hear. He had made it so much easier for her to cope and to understand what exactly was happening and why we were there.

Kelly feels Keith missed out on getting to know his new wife. They dated three weeks and suddenly she found herself married and praying for his safe return from the war. He tells her he really missed her good cooking.

Kelly became a stronger and more independent person. She was already pretty independent and never got a chance to become dependent on him. Her husband being away made her even stronger and made her prouder as an American and proud to serve her country as well. "That is why we all join the military because we love our country."

Kelly remembers getting together with other spouses and doing things together such as shopping, watching TV and sharing their feelings. She has made alot of lasting friendships and memories. "It takes someone very special to be a military wife, not everyone can do it," Kelly says. "A military wife has to be the mother and father, the main bread winner of the family, the backbone". You cannot fall apart. You need to be strong for the family.

Kelly believes the wife should stay strong, don't depend on your spouse too much because if they are in the military, they will deploy or go to war. She says that you have to have strength, faith, knowledge, and a great deal of patience. "Don't ever give up on your soldier. They need your support 125%."

Kathrin

Kathrin and her husband, Tom, have been married for 12 years. He has been in the Army since 1984. He recently served in Operation Iraqi Freedom from January 2003 until August 2003. He has recently retired and they welcomed a new baby girl, Emily, on June 25, 2004.

Kathrin recalls when President Bush declared war on Iraq. She was sitting will all her friends in front of the TV and although they all knew it was going to come to war, they still hoped that there would be another solution.

During his recent tour in Iraq she got to talk with him an average of about once to twice every month and received emails about every two weeks. He doesn't like to write letters and the whole time he was gone she only received ten letters.

Kathrin is actually use to the separations. Prior to his going to war he had just completed a one-year hardship tour in Korea. Needless to say, it didn't take her long to get back into the swing of things being by herself. She worked full time, went to school, and hung out with her friends. They were all in the same situation and supported each other. Kathrin was also the Family Readiness Group leader and was able to help the spouses who were struggling.

Kathrin feels her husband missed out on his son growing up. Over the past ten years he has spent four of those years away. Since retiring Katrin and Tom don't want to go through it again. Katrin made many new friends over the years and became a very strong woman.

One memory that sticks out in her mind the most is when Tom ordered her red roses over the internet for Valentines Day 2003. She remembers one of the nicest things he ever wrote her was that, "without me he would never be able to make it." "He thanked me for all the support I gave him."

Kathrin says you cannot sit and dwell on something you cannot change. Ask others how you can help them. Make new friends. Get together with your children. They miss daddy too. Find activities for them to keep their minds busy while Daddy is gone. If your spouse calls and he does not sound happy, don't take it personal.

Keep in mind that he is probably seeing things that are hard on him and he misses his family just as much as you miss him. Remember, every deployment has an end, and your soldier is waiting anxiously to come home to you.

My Story

In my late 20's I got a job working for the government on a military installation. I remember thinking all of my life that I would never marry a soldier because I knew what it did to my family and saw others struggle around me. I figured I could never do it anyway and then one day I saw this soldier walking down the sidewalk outside the building I worked in. I was never one to pursue a man but when I saw this man in uniform I struck up a conversation and the rest is history.

My husband has proudly served his country for 18 years in the U.S. Army. Right now we are stationed at Fort Eustis, Virginia where he is the Truck Master with the 155th Transportation Company. He served in Operation Desert SHIELD/STORM and recently in Operation Iraqi Freedom.

I can remember as a new military wife I felt helpless not knowing the ins and outs of the military. Trying to learn the language my husband spoke when he came home speaking the military lingo. I was always asking questions. As years passed I became more familiar with the Army way of life. There were things I did not like. For example, when a call would come in he would have to leave at that moment no matter what we were doing.

Understanding and making sacrifices are a big part of being a military wife. In the beginning I had a difficult time understanding why the Army came first and I came second. But as years passed I came to understand why. My husband was serving in the United States Army in the great land of America. It is his job, his duty, and he serves with pride. I have become a much stronger person and even more thankful for this country and the freedoms I have.

There have been struggles and times when I did not understand why things were happening. There have been times when he would pack his bags in a moment's notice and go away, whether it is for war or for a one year hardship tour overseas. But I've always dealt with it. I've had to take care of things here at home and take care of our son. Just him knowing I could take care of things at home made his job easier by not having to worry about us. He was going do a far greater job in defending our freedom.

I look back on the struggles we have overcome and see they have made us a stronger and closer family. My biggest adjustment was getting use to him being back home after a long tour of duty. Often a soldier will come home and just pick up where he left off. Don't get me wrong, it was great to have him home safe with us, but I had adjusted to being alone also. Things change and time passes so quickly. I felt my husband missed out on so much of our son's growing up. Our focus remains on making new memories and remaining close as a family.

Along with sacrifices comes frustration and loneliness with missed birthdays, anniversaries, and holidays. My husband is not a writer but he is full of surprises at times when I least expect it. He would much rather send a quick email or make a phone call. Lord knows I would not have made it through WWII as a military wife.

On our wedding anniversary this year he surprised me by sending me a dozen roses while he was serving in Operation Iraqi Freedom. How great is that in today's world of technology? When I would make a phone call to my husband I would hold my breath and pray to hear his voice say, "hello." Often I would hear the generators first in the background. I could hear him say, "Hang on" while he walked away to a quieter place.

On Valentines Day, 2004, I called my husband and there was no answer. Those times when he would not answer I would wonder what he was facing at that moment. I truly missed him. Valentines Day is one of the saddest holidays for a soldier to be away. Seeing couples in love, walking and holding hands, jewelry stores packed with men buying jewelry for their loved ones, vans filled with flowers driving up and down the streets, flowers everywhere. I was feeling pretty down that day not having my husband with me. I came home and checked my email and there was a picture from my soldier. He was holding a piece of paper with "Happy Valentines day, Patti" written on it with two hearts. That was the most romantic thing I ever saw. What a nice surprise. It was so good to see him well and thinking of me. It would not be long before he would call and ask if I had called. He wished me a Happy Valentine's Day and told me he loved me and missed me.

Little acts like that go along way. It makes the rough days better. I think back and think about the wives that never got to see pictures like that during the war. They received letters filled with emotions and strength from the soldier. We are so fortunate and actually spoiled in this age of war with today's way of communication.

Our son, Kyle, is just like his dad and does not like to write. So he and his dad would email each other or talked on the phone. We would get excited to see a letter or postcard arrive in the mail.

Dear Kyle,

How are you? I am doing very good. I miss you and mom alot. I am working hard so the time goes by quicker. I can't wait to come back home. We can go to the beaches and do some boogie boarding. We are going to have a good summer. I am glad to hear you are doing very well in school. That makes me very proud.

I will write again soon. I love and miss you very much,

Love Dad

NATIONAL ASSEMBLY BUILDING

Dear Patti & Kyle,

How are you? I am doing well. There is talk of coming back between the 15th of May and the 15th of June. Time is going very slow here and I can't wait to come back home. I miss you both very much. We have been pretty busy. It is starting to warm up—mid 80's during the day. I love you guys - be back soon

Ed

ALL RIGHTS RESERVED · PHOTOGRAPHY: MICHIEL SILLEM · DISTR. / PROD.: DOLPHIN COMPANY · TEL.: 4832642 · FAX: 4842642

SCENES OF KUWAIT

26 MAR 1998

Patti & Kyle Correa
118 Glenn Bryant rd
Hinesville, GA. 31313

While my soldier is deployed I get involved and help others. Performing acts of kindness is such a blessing and takes my mind off myself. It just makes you feel good to help others.

Wonderful and unexpected acts of kindness are often given by others when total strangers hear your spouse is at war and it makes you feel so proud when they say thanks to your soldier. I remember such an act that was bestowed on me while my husband was at war that I will never forget and now compels me to do random acts myself. I was on the phone with my hairdresser and, as most military wives know money is tight between paydays. I had had an emergency with my car and had to use the money that I was going to spend on my hair. While talking with my hairdresser, trying to cut corners where I could, I was unaware that another customer was listening to the conversation on her end. So I went into the salon and proceeded to get my hair done and when I was finished and ready to pay, my hairdresser said, "It is all taken care of." It took a few moments until I realized what had happened. Someone had paid for my haircut and highlights. I was like, "Wow! this is unbelievable, that a complete stranger would do this." She did it as a gesture of patriotism and to thank my husband for service to our country. Needless to say, tears began to fall down my cheek as well as everyone in the shop. There were many hugs that went around. To this day I do not know who that person was. That moment will forever be in my heart and encourage me to do random acts of kindness. It just makes your heart feel good. Oftentimes, I would be in a store and talking with a stranger in the checkout line and when I told them my soldier was away at war they would tell me to thank my soldier for them and that they are thankful for him and all our soldiers.

I am thankful to be an American and able to enjoy the freedoms that I have. I am very proud of our soldiers and that they fight for our freedom. Just listening to our national anthem makes me cry tears of pride for our country.

There are many sacrifices made as a military spouse. You have to put your career on hold, your dreams on hold. You have to raise your children while your soldier is away. YOU come last. There are also many rewards of being a military wife. The pride you feel for your soldier. Traveling all over the world, experiencing different lifestyles and cultures, making lasting friendships.

We currently live in military housing on base and I am often awoken by the morning bugle sound and later the sounds of soldiers' yelling cadence during their morning run. The pride I feel for our military is deep within my heart. I am thankful for those who serve and have given their lives to keep me free.

At the start of Operation Enduring Freedom, I was overwhelmed by the news media and could not stop watching. I knew my soldier would be leaving soon to go to war. On April 21, 2003 my husband left for Kuwait. The day he left I put on my second watch. You see, when he is deployed or at war where there is a time difference I set my second watch to his time. I do not take either watch off until he returns. That way, I feel closer to him.

As the war became more intense I was becoming so wrapped up

in the news it was eating away at my strength and focus that I needed to get through each day. Finally, I had to shut it off. When I did watch the news it was only to catch up and then I would turn it off and focus on other things that were more positive.

There were good days along the way and there were days of being lonely, frustrated, feeling as if no one cared. Often seemed like nothing went right. But then God would send a blessing my way just when I needed it. A friend would call just to say hi or someone from my church would call and check on me. I found when I was helping others it would take my mind off myself and my feelings. I made it and as I look back I am stronger because of what I went through.

While my husband was in Kuwait, I began each day with prayer to God to keep my soldier safe. A million thoughts went through my mind while he was at war. "Is he safe? Is he eating well? Is he warm at night? Does he think of me as much as I think of him? Are other military spouses thinking the same way I am?" Then I realized, "Yes, they are." Each day that went by I asked God not to take my soldier. I asked him to protect all the soldiers and give them peace in this time of war. I had to totally rely on God to get me through. He gives me the strength I need. There are challenges and sacrifices to be made but I faced each day with courage and hope that my soldier would come home safe to his family.

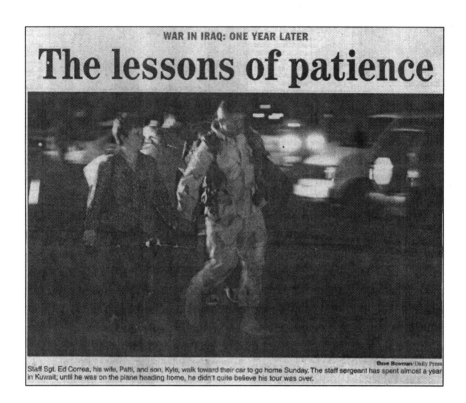

WAR IN IRAQ: ONE YEAR LATER

The lessons of patience

Dave Bowman/Daily Press

Staff Sgt. Ed Correa, his wife, Patti, and son, Kyle, walk toward their car to go home Sunday. The staff sergeant has spent almost a year in Kuwait; until he was on the plane heading home, he didn't quite believe his tour was over.

My soldier is home safe right now after serving in Kuwait. When I welcomed him home and hugged him it was as if time had stopped while in his arms. There are no guarantees he will not have to go back, but if he does we will face it with courage and strength and chalk it up as another challenge to overcome and new experiences in the life of a military family.

Dave Bowman/Daily Press

Staff Sgt. Ed Correa, based at Fort Eustis, is greeted by his wife, Patti, and son, Kyle, during Sunday's homecoming celebration.

Prayer for the Women

God,
Thank you for the relationships that we share throughout our life,
especially those we share within our military families. Help us to be
sensitive to each other's needs and give us the strength to face daily
challenges and sacrifices that are a part of the lifestyle we share.
May we continue to grow daily from a pebble to a rock on the home-
front. Help us to know the influence we have on others through our
smiles, touches, and acts of kindness. May we continue to give of
ourselves to our community. We thank you for all the blessings you
have bestowed upon us, and all the blessings that await us in the
future.

Glory to You

About the Author

Patti Correa is a military wife, a mother, and a friend to all she meets. Patti is living the roller coaster of emotions experienced by military wives. She is dedicated to sharing stories of hope, love, and survival from the homefront.

Patti's husband has been in the U.S. Army for 18 years. They currently live in Virginia where her husband is stationed at Fort Eustis in Newport News. They have a 16 year old son, Kyle, and dog, Casey.

Patti has begun working on her next two books. She is seeking stories from wives, mothers, and daughters of soldiers who have served from WWII to present-day war. The second book will focus on the children from ages five to 18 and their stories of coping and dealing with mom or dad being away.

Contact Patti at pbl2rock@hotmail.com and tell her your story.

Pebble;
An irregular, crinkled or grainy surface…

Rock;
Foundation, support, refuge, a Gem…

(Merriam-Webster Online Dictionary)